CREATE KILLER CONTENT!

CREATE KILLER CONTENT!

Master the art of customer-centric marketing

MARCIA HYLTON

Copyright © 2023 Marcia Hylton
All rights reserved.
ISBN: 9798388128805

For those who have faced seemingly insurmountable obstacles yet found a way to dream big and to all those who opened doors to make finding our way possible.

Contents

Preface ix
Introduction xi

STEP 1: Getting Ready

Chapter 1: Gather Your Tools 3
Chapter 2: Allocate Time 7
Chapter 3: Dedicate Time 11

STEP 2: Information Gathering

Chapter 4: Gain Insight 17
Chapter 5: Uncover What's Relevant 23
Chapter 6: Maximize Repurposing 29
Chapter 7: A Cohesive Plan 37

STEP 3: Content Creation

Chapter 8: Speak Their Language 45
Chapter 9: Get Keyword Smart 59
Chapter 10: Write with Purpose 65
Chapter 11: Autopilot & Efficiency 73

Appendix A: Your 11-Step Roadmap 80
Appendix B: Best Practices 83

Preface

As a passionate advocate for the growth of small businesses, I'm on a mission to help them thrive in today's competitive marketplace. Having worked as a marketing strategist for Fortune 500 companies and owning my own marketing agency, I've seen firsthand how challenging it can be for small business owners to compete with more prominent brands.

That's why I wrote this book – to empower small business owners to take charge of their marketing and engage in strategic content marketing. With my expertise and practical tips, you'll learn how to create compelling content that resonates with your ideal prospects, plan and schedule your content for maximum impact, and measure your results to improve your marketing efforts continuously.

I know that every small business owner deserves to succeed, and strategic content marketing is critical to achieving that success. With this concise and actionable guide, I'm confident you'll have the knowledge and tools to take your marketing efforts to the next level.

So, let's dive in together and unlock the power of strategic content marketing! I'm excited to share the lessons I've picked up through the years with you and help you achieve the success you deserve.

Introduction

Have you struggled to create content that truly resonates with your audience? If so, you've come to the right place! I'm excited to introduce my book, Create Killer Content, a comprehensive guide to creating audience-driven, client-attracting content.

As someone who has spent years working in the marketing industry, I've seen countless businesses struggle with their marketing efforts. I created this book – to help business owners and marketers understand the importance of strategic content marketing and provide practical tips and tools to help you create content that genuinely connects with your audience.

Inside the book, I'll dive into the art of content creation, starting with ideal client clarity and how to research and create content that meets their needs. I'll also explore the power of repurposing your content and how to optimize it across multiple channels. Additionally, I'll discuss the importance of planning, time management, and keyword research to ensure your content is optimized for search engines.

At the heart of this book is the idea of developing a content strategy based on your ideal client's needs, so you can create content that resonates with them and ultimately drives business growth. Whether you're a seasoned content creator or just starting, this book is packed with tips, tricks, and strategies to help create content that engages and inspires your audience.

So, if you're ready to take your content marketing to the next level, let's dive in, take charge of your marketing, and create killer content!

GETTING READY

STEP 1

It's easy to want to ignore this step because here is where we discuss time management and other non-marketing topics. But here's the thing, we all have distractions and competing priorities.

If we don't take specific action to lock in periods to get your marketing done, your marketing will be more tactics than strategy. You'll post aimlessly as most small business owners do and not strategically like most don't.

I know your business is important to you. You didn't start a business to fail, but winning requires focus, commitment, and strategic action. It's a win-win for you to market thoughtfully because just by doing that, you will be doing more and better than 65% of business owners and will serve your clients better.

CHAPTER ONE

Gather Your Tools

Are you ready to take your content marketing to the next level? Before we dive into the nitty-gritty details of content creation and strategy, it's essential to take a step back and prepare for the work ahead.

In this first chapter, I'll discuss the importance of mentally preparing yourself for the work ahead and setting aside time to focus on your content marketing efforts. I'll provide a link to download a free editorial calendar to help you organize your content strategy and maximize your time.

By preparing and getting organized, you'll be better equipped to learn from the rest of the book and take action on the strategies outlined. Whether you're a seasoned content creator or just starting, this chapter is an essential first step toward creating a successful content marketing strategy.

So, take a deep breath, clear your mind, and get ready to dive into the world of strategic content marketing. With the right mindset and tools, you'll be well on your way to creating content that engages your audience and drives business growth.

You've already taken your first big step by getting this book — **a strategic marketing planner and guide.**

Your next step, grabbing a copy of a free editorial calendar template, is equally essential because the eCal and this book work best when used side-by-side.

Why work from an editorial calendar for content development?

An editorial calendar is a must-have tool if you want to create content that engages your audience and aligns with your overall business goals.

An editorial calendar can provide many benefits for businesses and content creators. Here are a few key advantages:

- Improved organization
- Increased efficiency
- Better collaboration
- Enhanced audience engagement

Before we begin, let's gather the tools you'll need. Think of this as similar to your prep time when following a recipe. You'll need to be in the right frame of mind, so make sure you're in a space where you can get in the zone and remain focused.

- A block of time set aside to do these initial steps
- A copy of the eCal template
- Your daily calendar
- Your laptop

Other tools that can help with creating an editorial calendar:

- Hubspot
- Trello
- Airtable
- Asana
- Hootsuite

The eCal Template

Your eCal will include the topics and themes you plan to cover, your timeline for covering each topic, and the type of content you'll create for each. But that's just the beginning! To ensure that you stay on track, be sure to set deadlines for each piece of content and account for all the research, writing, editing, and design work that goes into creating it.

But it's not just about creating content – you must have a strategic approach to using it! You'll plan out your marketing strategy in advance, align that with your overall business goals, and include a column for analytics (KPIs) to track your content's performance and measure your success.

And if you're working with a team, assign responsibilities and clarify each team member's role in the content development process.

But even working solo (which many of my clients do), with all these elements, you'll create a comprehensive content development plan that drives engagement and achieves your business goals.

So don't wait. Let's start planning your editorial calendar today to develop your content strategy!

> Your next step — making a copy of the eCal template (free) — is equally essential because it's one of the ways you will make this book work for you.

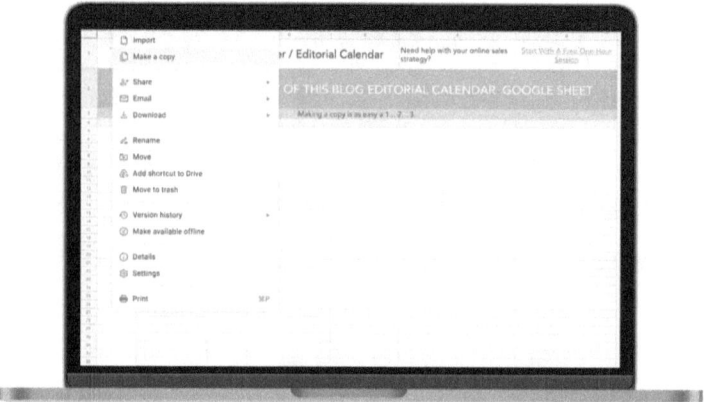

Download your free copy of the eCal template

Make Your Copy

You can easily copy the *forever-free editorial calendar template* from this URL

http://ecal.marciahylton.com

Here's How to Make Your Copy

To create a copy of this template, go to the URL above, then on the Google Sheets menu bar, **choose FILE >> MAKE A COPY**. A copy of the template will then be saved to your Google Sheets. I suggest adding it to your browser bookmarks so you won't have difficulty locating your version later. But if you do, you can always return to the URL above and make a new copy of the template. It's forever free to you.

Now that you have this guide and your very own copy of the eCal template, it's time to organize and create a content strategy and develop relevant content.

CHAPTER TWO

Allocate Time

As a business owner, time is one of your most precious resources, and finding time for content creation can be a challenge. However, by conducting a time inventory, you can better understand how you spend your time and identify areas where you can free up time for content creation.

In this chapter, I'll guide you through conducting a time inventory, which involves tracking your activities for a while, typically a week or two. By analyzing your time inventory, you can identify areas where you're spending time that could be redirected to content creation, such as reducing time spent on administrative tasks or social media.

By being realistic about what needs to be removed from your calendar to make time for content creation, you'll be better equipped to commit to a content creation schedule that works for you. In the next chapter, I'll discuss the importance of committing to a schedule and provide tips for maximizing your dedicated content creation time.

So, let's conduct a time inventory and unlock the time you need to create effective and strategic marketing content!

Do A Quick Time Inventory

Strategic content creation can be time-consuming, but creating a time inventory helps manage your schedule so you can stay committed to your content creation responsibilities. **Here are the steps you can follow to make a time inventory:**

1. Record your activities

Start by recording all your activities for a week. This includes work, commuting, personal activities, and leisure time. Write down how long you spend on each activity and at what time.

2. Categorize your activities

Next, categorize your activities into work, family, personal, and leisure time groups.

3. Identify time wasters

Look at your activities and identify any time wasters. This could be social media, excessive TV watching, or spending too much time on tasks that aren't important.

4. Determine your priorities

Identify your priorities and decide how much time you want to spend on each category of activities. For example, you might spend one hour daily on content creation.

5. Schedule your time

Use a scheduling tool to create a plan for your time. This could be a calendar, planner, or scheduling app. Create a block for each activity you're responsible for completing.

6. Review and adjust

Review your time inventory regularly and adjust as needed. This will help you stay on track and use your time effectively.

Try Time Blocking

Time blocking is a time management technique that involves scheduling specific tasks and activities into designated time slots throughout the day. This method aims to help individuals be more productive, focused, and efficient by allocating a particular amount of time for each task and minimizing distractions.

Time blocking encourages people to prioritize their tasks and allows them to have a clear understanding of their daily workload. Here's how it works:

1. **List your tasks**

Write down all the tasks you need to accomplish, including personal and professional ones. This list will give you an overview of what needs to be done and help you prioritize.

2. **Prioritize tasks**

Sort the tasks by importance and urgency. This process will help you identify which tasks must be completed first and which can be postponed or delegated.

3. **Estimate time for each task**

Determine how long each task is likely to take. Be realistic in your estimation, as overestimating or underestimating can negatively impact your schedule.

4. **Schedule your time blocks**

Divide your day into blocks of time dedicated to specific tasks. These time blocks can range from 15 minutes to several hours, depending on the task's complexity and your personal preference. Make sure to include breaks and buffer time for unexpected interruptions.

5. Stick to the schedule

Once you have created your time-blocked schedule, follow it as closely as possible. Stay focused during each time block, and avoid multitasking or getting distracted.

6. Review and adjust

Review your progress at the end of each day and adjust your schedule as needed for the next day. This review process helps you identify areas of improvement and make necessary changes to increase your productivity.

Benefits of time blocking include:

Improved focus and productivity: Time blocking encourages you to concentrate on one task at a time, reducing multitasking and increasing overall productivity.

Better work-life balance: By scheduling personal and professional tasks, time blocking allows you to maintain a healthy balance between work and personal life.

Reduced stress: Knowing what needs to be done and when it will be completed can alleviate stress related to an overwhelming workload.

Greater sense of accomplishment: As you complete tasks within their designated time blocks, you can feel a sense of achievement, motivating you to continue being productive.

Enhanced time management skills: Time blocking helps you become more aware of how you spend your time, allowing you to use it better in the future.

CHAPTER THREE

Dedicate Time

This chapter will explore the essential strategies for managing your time effectively and ensuring you have the resources to create high-quality marketing content. From time inventory to time blocking, I'll cover everything you need to know to maximize your productivity and achieve your content goals.

I'll start by discussing the importance of time inventory, which involves assessing your available time for content creation and determining where your time is best spent. I'll also explore the concept of time blocking, which involves setting aside specific blocks of time for different tasks, allowing you to focus your energy and attention on creating content.

Additionally, I'll discuss the benefits of committing to a schedule, which can help you stay on track and progress toward your content goals. I'll also share practical tips for distributing sections of the work over several days, enabling you to tackle larger projects and break them down into manageable tasks.

By the end of this chapter, you'll have a solid understanding of how to schedule and commit time for content creation, ensuring you have the resources and focus on creating high-quality marketing content that drives engagement and conversions. So, let's dive in and explore the world of time management for content creation!

Schedule Research Days

If you haven't already done so, complete your time inventory to commit periods for content planning, research, and creation. I promise you'll be glad you did.

Once you've completed your time inventory, open your calendar and identify the exact dates, number of hours, days of the week, and frequency you'll commit to doing the research that helps you discover post ideas that will address your ideal client's needs.

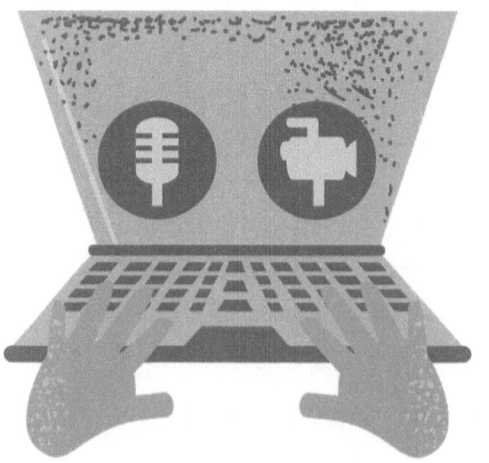

I recommend booking *quarterly sessions* with yourself, with several hours dedicated to researching your content topics. Once you've decided, put it into your calendar as a repeat event, then set automatic reminders to ensure it gets done.

Schedule Writing Days

So, if you're struggling to find time to create content like most of us, here's a helpful tip. Look at your calendar and set aside a few hours each month to draft the copy for your planned posts for the upcoming month. Deciding on a specific block of time for each draft is essential, considering your sales goals and how many posts you want to write.

I recommend scheduling your draft creation sessions for the first week of each month to simplify this process and dedicating the following week to finalizing your posts. Block out the necessary days and times for these tasks as repeat events on your calendar and set automated reminders to keep you on track.

By following this approach, you'll have the chance to consider different perspectives, evaluate your writing, and develop your ideas before publishing each post. Ultimately, this will help you create high-quality content that resonates with your audience. So what are you waiting for? Start scheduling your content creation!

Schedule Posting Days

So, if you want to maximize your sales and product launches with your content posts? Then listen up!

For best results, it's essential to plan your posting dates around your overall sales goals or upcoming product launches for the following month. This will allow you to promote your products and reach monthly sales targets.

To make things even easier, most content platforms have a nifty feature that allows you to schedule and publish posts automatically. So all you need to do is open up your calendar, choose the planned dates and times for each piece of content, and set up automated reminders to give your post a final once-over before it goes live. With this approach, you'll be able to stay on top of your content schedule and ensure your posts align with your sales and marketing strategy. So give it a try and watch your sales soar!

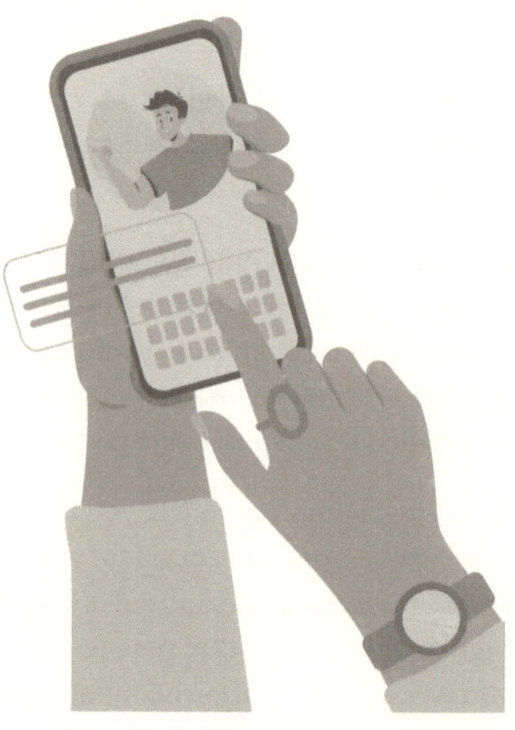

INFORMATION GATHERING

STEP

2

Research and information gathering is critical to developing compelling content. This is the step that many businesses miss. They instead rely on guessing or their best instinct.

But here's the thing, you can have great instincts and still get this wrong. To know how to get there, first learn where there is, then use the tools available to take the most efficient path.

If you want to have clarity about your ideal client and their pain points, don't guess. There are tools available to help. Ask or research.

CHAPTER FOUR

Gain Insight

Dedicate your research sessions to learning about and documenting the types of content your ideal client craves and identifying the solutions they need. As you research, open the editorial calendar template to track and manage your content ideas and tie them into your product sales plans.

If you haven't done so, your first action is to download the eCal planner and template. *Please revisit the "Get Organized" section for guidance on how to make a copy of the template.*

No more guessing. It's essential to make time for research. Without this step, you are essentially shooting in the dark without knowing if your ideal client is interested in your chosen topic.

> The time wasted by skipping the research step leads to lost opportunities, and ultimately results in lost revenue.

Research isn't glamorous. It isn't sexy but can make a difference between making millions and earning far less revenue.

Let's start by getting to know your ideal client. And "ideal client" means the exact person you want to serve with your products.

Ideal Client Persona

As a business owner, understanding your ideal client is essential for creating effective marketing strategies, nurturing long-term relationships, and driving growth. However, identifying your ideal client can be a daunting task.

- **Who are they?**
- **What motivates them?**
- **What are their pain points?**

In the following pages, I'll explore creating an ideal client persona that captures the essence of your ideal customer. I'll have you ask yourself several questions to help you gain clarity on who your ideal client is, such as their demographics, values, goals, challenges, and interests. By the end of this chapter, you'll have a crystal-clear picture of your ideal client, enabling you to create targeted marketing messages and build relationships that resonate with their needs and desires.

Remember, you can't help someone whose pain points you don't know or understand. That's why creating an ideal client persona is crucial for identifying the pain points of your target audience and providing solutions that address their unique challenges. I'll share an example persona to give you a sense of what *your* ideal client persona could look like.

However, it's important to remember that your ideal client persona should be unique to you based on your specific business goals and product offers. So, let's start creating your ideal client persona and unlocking the power of targeted strategic marketing!

Ask Yourself

To create content that converts, you need to start by clarifying who you're serving. Saying "everyone" might seem safe, but it's not the most effective approach.

Trying to serve everyone is the same as serving no one at all.

If you want your marketing language to resonate with your potential buyers, you must clearly define who you want to reach.

Don't worry, though – I've got your back. *Visit my website and download my ideal client workbook* to help you get the extreme clarity that's possible to have as you create killer content.

In the meantime, here are a few questions you should ask yourself.

1. Can I put into words who my perfect client is?
2. What is a problem they have that I can solve?
3. How can I use my expertise to help them solve this problem?
4. How can my product/service help them solve their problems?
5. What kind of content do they enjoy consuming?

6. What kind of language and tone will resonate with them?
7. What does my ideal client want to know or have?
8. What does my ideal client want to feel?
9. What solution is my ideal client seeking?
10. What questions are my ideal client asking?
11. Where online does my ideal client typically look for solutions?
12. Where is my ideal client actively engaged and asking questions?
13. Which experts do my ideal client go to for answers?
14. How can I personalized responses to comments or direct messages?
15. How can I be more thoughtful in replying to customer reviews or feedback?
16. How can I create interactive content that encourages participation and discussion?
17. How can I engage in authentic storytelling that connects with my audience's emotions and values?

Once you've answered these questions, you'll be well on your way to creating compelling content that converts. Think of it this way, **if you know me, you'll know what to say to capture my interest.** So, work through these questions and begin getting extreme clarity. I've enclosed a simple persona example on the next page.

Ideal Client Persona

- **Name:** JACQUELINE
- **Age:** 35
- **Job:** Physician
- **Location:** Normal, IL
- **Income:** $175,000
- **Other:** married with one child.

- Values: Her faith, family, career, and contribution to society

- Goals: Boost sales of her products & services and retire early

- Fears: Not having free time to travel and spend with her child.

- Challenges: Trying to lower her clinic's job turnover rates

- Hobbies: Golfing, writing her blog, traveling

- Pain Points: Jacqueline wants to grow her ten-year-old private practice but doesn't know how to market her services or sell her products effectively. She is also finding it challenging to get clarity on her ideal client. Jacque spends numerous hours creating and posting away and not seeing the results she wants.

- Status: She is willing and ready to invest in her business growth.

Create Your Own

- Name: _____
- Age: _____
- Job: _____
- Location: _____
- Income: $_____
- Other: _____

- Values:

- Goals:

- Fears:

- Challenges:

- Hobbies:

- Pain Points:

- Status:

CHAPTER FIVE

Uncover What's Relevant

Welcome to the fascinating realm of researching and curating content that resonates with your ideal prospects! In this chapter, I'll dive into the art and science of discovering your target audience's questions, concerns, and interests, ensuring that your marketing efforts speak directly to their needs and desires. Keeping your ideal buyers at the forefront of your content strategy will create a powerful connection with your audience and pave the way for long-term success.

I'll explore various online tools and resources that can help you uncover valuable insights into your prospects' online behavior, from the questions they ask and the comments they post to the information sources they trust. These tools will empower you to tailor your content to address their pain points and spark curiosity.

Moreover, this chapter will guide you through the process of brainstorming ideas based on your research findings, helping you develop a content plan that captures the attention of your target market. I'll discuss using these insights to create content that informs, entertains, and compels your prospects to take action.

So, get ready to embark on a journey of discovery as we unlock the secrets of crafting relevant and engaging marketing content that captivates your ideal buyers and drives your business forward!

Finding Compelling Topics

Once you've got a crystal clear picture of your ideal client, it's time to start figuring out how to solve their problems. And the key to doing that is knowing how they ask for what they want and where they're looking for solutions.

Even if your ideal client doesn't always know what they need, they usually know what they want. And that's where you come in. Your goal is to find out what they want and then provide them with what they need to solve their problems.

By doing this, you create opportunities to help each client resolve multiple issues while increasing your sales at the same time – talk about a win-win situation!

So, let's start connecting with your ideal client in a new way — focusing on *their* wants and needs. Doing this builds lasting relationships and drives your business forward.

Tools to help you research and improve your content quality

These tools and strategies help you get inside the mind of your ideal client. Want to know what their concerns are? Want to know what questions they ask? Want to know what features and products they are seeking? This is where you start—no more relying on best guesses that lead to pointless, aimless posting. Now **you can build from knowing** what is genuinely appealing to your prospects.

A few great places to begin researching content marketing topics

- Search and download findings using trends.google.com
- Engage in social listening on Facebook threads/discussions
- Regularly review answerthepublic.com
- Track relevant discussions on quora.com
- Set up and use an account with SEMrush

Using these tools to help ensure the content you create is of value to the prospects you want to attract to your business and who will eventually become brand advocates.

- **Google Scholar:** An excellent resource for finding scholarly literature and reliable research sources.
- **WolframAlpha:** A powerful computational search engine and knowledge base for exploring data and doing calculations.
- **Twitter:** An excellent source for finding news and updates on your research topics.
- **Reddit:** A forum for finding and discussing topics with a large community of knowledgeable people.
- **Google Alerts:** Set up an alert for your topic and get notified when new content is posted.
- **SurveyMonkey:** Conduct surveys to gain insights into topics you're researching.
- **BuzzSumo:** Discover the most shared content related to your topic.
- **AHREFS:** A comprehensive tool for researching and analyzing backlinks and keywords.

Brainstorming Content

Once you've researched, you may also want to brainstorm additional ideas based on your findings. Here are several brainstorming tools to choose from.

- **MindMeister:** a tremendous online brainstorming tool that allows you to create mind maps to help you organize your thoughts and ideas.
- **IdeaFlip:** a great brainstorming tool that helps you quickly generate and organize ideas.
- **Realtime Board:** a powerful brainstorming and collaboration tool that helps teams capture, organize, and share ideas in real-time.
- **Mural:** a cloud-based brainstorming and collaboration tool that helps teams capture, organize, and share ideas visually.
- **StormBoard:** an online collaboration and brainstorming tool that helps teams collaborate and share ideas quickly and easily.
- **MindUp:** an online brainstorming and collaboration tool that helps teams capture, organize, and share ideas visually.
- **AYOA:** a powerful brainstorming and collaboration tool that helps teams capture, organize, and share ideas quickly and easily.
- **TeamGantt:** an online brainstorming and collaboration tool that helps teams capture, organize, and interactively share ideas.
- **IdeaJam:** an excellent online brainstorming and collaboration tool that helps teams capture, organize, and share ideas quickly and easily.
- **Trello:** a great online collaboration and brainstorming tool that helps teams organize, prioritize, and track ideas in real-time.

Brainstorming content can be incredibly helpful once you have done some research on the needs of your ideal client. After all, creating content for the sake of creating content is not effective. You need to ensure that your content resonates with your audience and addresses their pain points.

One way to do this is to brainstorm various angles or perspectives that your content can take. For example, if your ideal client is a small business owner, you could brainstorm content ideas that focus on their unique challenges or common misconceptions about running a small business. By taking a different angle or approach, you can create content that stands out from the crowd and truly resonates with your audience.

Another helpful way to brainstorm content is to think about what questions your ideal client may have. This can be particularly useful if you are creating educational or informative content. By answering your ideal client's questions, you can establish yourself as an authority in your niche and build trust with your audience.

Overall, brainstorming content is a crucial step in the content creation process. It allows you to get creative and come up with ideas that will truly resonate with your audience. By taking the time to brainstorm content ideas and approaches, you can create content that is both impactful and effective.

CHAPTER SIX

Maximize Repurposing

This chapter will explore the art and science of strategically repurposing your marketing content across different channels and formats, maximizing its reach and impact. By repurposing content, you can extend its lifespan, reach new audiences, and reinforce your brand message in various ways.

I'll discuss the benefits of repurposing your content, from saving time and resources to boosting your search engine optimization (SEO) efforts. I'll also explore ways to repurpose your content, such as turning blog posts into social media graphics or transforming customer testimonials into case studies.

Moreover, I'll provide practical tips and examples of how to repurpose content, including an example of a vlog post that was repurposed in two ways - an Instagram carousel and a marketing email. You'll see firsthand how repurposing can breathe new life into your content and help you achieve your marketing goals.

So, if you're ready to take your marketing content to the next level, grab a cup of coffee, sit back, and let's explore the world of content repurposing!

Why Repurpose Content

If you're like most of us, you're struggling to keep up with your content creation schedule. You may also feel like you're constantly churning out new content, only to see it buried and forgotten by your followers. The truth is, creating new content from scratch can be a time-consuming and exhausting process.

That's where content repurposing comes in.

> Repurposing content means presenting existing content in a new format or for a new platform.
>
> And the best part? It won't hurt! In fact, repurposing your content can help you reach a wider audience and get more mileage out of your hard work.

Think about it – not all of your followers see every post. By repurposing your content, you can present it in new and exciting ways that catch the attention of different segments of your audience. And when you repurpose your content for other platforms – such as turning a blog post into a video or a podcast – you can reach even more people and drive more engagement with your brand.

So don't let your hard work go to waste! Repurpose your content and watch it work harder for you. I'll show you how to do just that on the next page and again later in the book – with practical tips, tricks, and strategies to help you get the most out of your content.

Ways To Repurpose A Blog

1. Create a podcast episode based on the blog post content or vice-versa.
2. Turn a blog post into a video or series of videos.
3. Transform the blog post into a webinar or online course, or vice-versa.
4. Use one-liner excerpts from the blog post (or podcast) as social media posts with a link to the original post.
5. Convert the blog post into an infographic or other visual content.
6. Create an e-book or white paper based on the blog post, a client interaction, or a podcast transcript.
7. Use the blog post as the basis for a live event or workshop.
8. Repurpose the blog post as a guest post on another blog or publication (e.g., LinkedIn.)
9. Use the blog post as the basis for a press release or media pitch.
10. Turn the blog post into a slide presentation for sharing on platforms like SlideShare.

By repurposing each piece of content in these ways, you have now 10x-ed your content and can capture a wider audience and drive more engagement with your brand. It's essential to keep your ideal client in mind and ensure that the content remains relevant to their interests and needs when repurposing your content.

Additionally, optimizing the repurposed content for each channel is crucial, adjusting the format and tone as needed to ensure it resonates with your audience.

e.g., Blog post repurposed

Post: Benefits of Having Custom Cakes At Your Child's Birthday Party

Custom cakes can add an extra touch of magic to your child's birthday party. They are impressive centerpieces and can also be designed to fit your child's personality and interests. Here are some benefits of choosing a custom cake for your child's next birthday party.

First, a custom cake can be tailored to your child's interests. Whether they love unicorns, sports, or a particular cartoon character, a custom cake can incorporate these interests into the design. This level of personalization can make your child feel special and loved on their special day.

Secondly, custom cakes can be designed to fit the party's overall theme. Whether you're throwing a princess party or a superhero party, a custom cake can be designed to perfectly complement the theme, making your child's birthday party feel cohesive and memorable.

Finally, a custom cake can be a unique way to celebrate your child's milestones. Whether it's their first birthday or sweet sixteen, a custom cake can help to mark these special occasions and create lasting memories.

Repurposed as an Instagram carousel

1. Custom cakes can add an extra touch of magic to your child's birthday party!
2. Tailor the cake to your child's interests with a custom design they will love.
3. A custom cake can be designed to fit the overall theme of your child's party, making it feel extra special and cohesive.
4. Celebrate your child's milestones with a custom cake they'll remember for years.

5. Make your child's birthday party unique and special with a custom cake designed just for them!

Repurposed as a marketing email: Make Your Child's Birthday Extra Magical with a Custom Cake.

Hey there!

Are you planning a birthday party for your little one? We've got a fantastic idea to make their special day even more magical: Custom cakes! Our recent blog post, "Benefits of Having Custom Cakes at Your Child's Birthday Party," explains why a custom cake is a perfect addition to any celebration. Here's a quick rundown of the top benefits:

1. Personalized for your child's interests. Is your child obsessed with unicorns or crazy about soccer? Custom cakes can be tailored to showcase their unique interests, making them feel extra special on their big day!
2. It fits the party theme like a glove. Whether you're hosting a princess or superhero-themed party, a custom cake can be designed to perfectly complement the theme, tying everything together for a truly unforgettable experience.
3. Celebrate milestones in a memorable way. From their first birthday to their sweet sixteen, custom cakes help mark those precious milestones and create lasting memories you and your child will cherish forever.

Ready to add a touch of magic to your child's birthday party with a custom cake? Check out our full blog post for more inspiration, or get in touch with us to discuss your dream cake design!

Wishing you a day filled with sweet moments,
[Your Name / Your Business Name]

More In-Depth Ways to Repurpose Content

One piece of content can serve you multiple times by becoming the source of various posts for a variety of marketing platforms:

Create social media posts: Take critical points from your copy-heavy content and turn them into social media captions or tweets. You can also create graphics or videos to accompany your posts.

Make a video or podcast: Take the main ideas from your blog post and turn them into a video or podcast. This allows you to reach a different audience who may prefer consuming content in another format.

Create an infographic: If you have a blog post containing a lot of data or statistics, turn them into an infographic. This is a great way to visualize complex information and make it more shareable.

Write an email newsletter: Use your blog post to inspire your following email newsletter. Summarize the main ideas and include a link back to your blog post.

Create a lead magnet: If your content covers a topic your audience is highly interested in, turn it into a lead magnet. This could be a free guide, checklist, or template your audience can download in exchange for their email address.

Turn it into a webinar or live stream: If a blog post covers a complex topic or provides valuable insights, consider turning it into a webinar or live stream. This lets you interact with your audience in real-time and answer their questions.

Create an ebook: If you have a series of related content (blog posts, for instance), consider turning them into an ebook. This can be a great lead magnet or a way to monetize your content.

Republish it on other platforms: Don't be afraid to republish your blog post on other platforms, such as Medium or LinkedIn. Just make sure to include a link back to your website. This can help elevate your site's ranking in search engines (SEO).

Make a slide deck: Use your content as a foundation for a presentation slide deck or an Instagram carousel. This is a great way to summarize the main points and make your content visually appealing.

Create a case study: If your content provides insights or success stories, consider turning it into a case study. This is a great way to showcase your expertise and build trust with your audience.

Revive an older post: If a post is over four months old and was well-liked by your audience, update the visual and post that item again.

CHAPTER SEVEN

A Cohesive Plan

Now that you clearly understand your ideal client and have identified their interests, pain points, and preferred channels, it's time to develop a strategy that will enable you to reach and engage with them effectively.

This chapter will explore various strategies for driving traffic, boosting engagement, and increasing conversions, including link, repurposing, and ad strategies. These strategies are built upon the insights gained in previous chapters, enabling you to develop a cohesive and effective marketing plan that aligns with your business goals.

I'll provide practical tips and examples for creating each strategy, ensuring you have the tools and knowledge to take your marketing efforts to the next level. By the end of this chapter, you'll clearly understand how to create a comprehensive marketing strategy tailored to your ideal client's needs and preferences. So, let's dive in and start drafting your winning marketing strategy!

Consolidate Your Findings Into A Strategic Content Plan

Once you have created your lists, put all your research into the editorial calendar. You will be counting on the repetitive use of this invaluable resource.

Plug dates beside each topic. Your dates should align with your overall business plan (including product launches and announcements).

For example, if you're a baker planning to launch a new cake around the start of the holiday season, you would plan to write one or two relevant blog posts in the four preceding weeks and begin repurposing that content.

Consolidating this gives you a framework for graphics, captions, blog posts, and other marketing content. You will eventually turn this into a plan of action to strategically appeal t your ideal prospects and direct them to your business's products or services.

e.g., aligning your content strategy with your business goals

Carla was excited to launch her new line of organic skincare products but unsure how to create buzz around it. After attending a marketing seminar, she realized the importance of content marketing in today's digital age. She began researching her target audience and their interests, learning that many were environmentally conscious and looking for sustainable options.

With this information in mind, Carla crafted a content marketing strategy aligned with her business goals. She created a blog that featured articles on the benefits of using organic skincare, the impact of chemicals in beauty products on the environment, and the story behind her company's mission.

Carla used keyword research to optimize her blog for search engines to ensure her content reached the right audience. She also shared her blog posts on social media and repurposed them into email newsletters to keep her subscribers engaged.

The result was a surge in organic traffic to her website and increased product inquiries. Carla's content marketing strategy not only helped her reach her target audience but also positioned her brand as an industry leader in the organic skincare market.

By aligning her content marketing strategy with her business goals and understanding her audience's needs and interests, Carla created a compelling story that resonated with her audience and drove business growth.

Create A Link Strategy

One powerful way to boost your sales and product launches is strategically using hyperlinks within your blog posts and web pages.

Think of hyperlinks as bridges that connect your site to others and vice versa. By linking to relevant sites that serve a similar audience as yours, you can improve your search engine rankings for important keywords. So how do you create a winning link strategy?

Your first step is identifying and developing a potential partner site database. Look for non-competitor sites that share your target audience and try to find win-win opportunities with other business owners.

Next, you'll want to research and identify trustworthy, reputable partner sites that can help you earn the trust of your site visitors. Look for opportunities to link to these sites within relevant blog posts and webpage copy.

Finally, don't forget to identify relevant products you can promote by interlining them throughout your website. Plan out the placement of links to these products and include them strategically in your content.

Following these steps, you can create a powerful link strategy that supports your sales goals, helps you rank in search results, and drives traffic to your site.

Create A Reuse Strategy

Repurposing your top-performing organic content is a powerful way to extend its reach across multiple channels.

Start by analyzing your organic content's engagement metrics and identifying the pieces that have generated the most interest. Then, think about how you can repurpose them to reach new audiences.

For example, you might turn a blog post into a social media graphic or a podcast episode into a video clip.

Repurposing content can save time and resources by creating new content from existing material. It can also reinforce your brand message by delivering it in different formats and platforms, generating ongoing engagement and loyalty.

So, consider developing a repurposing strategy based on your top-performing organic content to maximize the impact of your marketing efforts.

Create An Ad Strategy

The key to a successful ad strategy is to identify content that performs well organically and then leverage it to drive paid traffic. To do this, you need to analyze your organic content's engagement metrics, such as likes, shares, and comments, and identify the pieces that have generated the most interest.

Once you've identified your top-performing content, you can use it as a blueprint for your ad strategy. By amplifying your successful organic content with paid ads, you can reach a wider audience and drive even more engagement and conversions. Moreover, you can use the insights gained from your organic content's performance to optimize your ad targeting and messaging, ensuring you're reaching the right audience with the right message.

The benefits of planning an ad strategy around your top-performing organic content are clear. It allows you to maximize your return on investment by targeting content that has already resonated with your audience, reducing the risk of ad fatigue, and ensuring that your message is impactful and effective. Moreover, it enables you to build a cohesive content strategy that aligns with your overall marketing goals, establishing a solid brand identity and fostering long-term customer relationships.

CONTENT CREATION

STEP

3

The art of persuasion is at the heart of effective marketing, and your choice of words or visuals can make or break your campaign.

In a world where information is available at our fingertips, and attention spans are shrinking, it's crucial to stand out by crafting compelling content that resonates with your target audience.

This section of the book will delve into the vital elements of creating captivating marketing communication, focusing on search engine optimization (SEO), emotional power words, crafting headlines for blogs, and writing marketing emails.

CHAPTER EIGHT

Speak Their Language

Before you can compel your prospects to buy, you need to harness the power of words to create captivating marketing communication.

Emotional power words are the secret sauce that can turn your content from ordinary to extraordinary. These words evoke strong emotions and connect with your audience on a deeper level, ultimately driving them to take action.

Incorporating emotional power words into your marketing communication can enhance engagement, encourage sharing, and improve conversion rates.

By understanding and mastering the importance of compelling prospects with your choice of words in your marketing communication, you'll be well on your way to creating a powerful and effective marketing strategy. This chapter aims to equip you with the tools and insights necessary to craft content that captures attention and leaves a lasting impression on your audience.

Appeal To Emotion

BASIC TYPES OF EMOTIONAL POWER WORDS

Use emotionally powerful words in your content, including blog posts and headlines. Make an emotional appeal or build curiosity.

- Fear Power Words
- Encouragement Power Words
- Lust Power Words
- Anger Power Words
- Greed Power Words
- Safety Power Words
- Forbidden Power Words

Example: "She *was in so much agony...*"

The word agony is a careful word choice and conveys a level of distress that most can empathize with.

Power Words & Phrases

In marketing, emotional words convey a brand's personality and values, establish a connection with its target audience and create a memorable brand experience.

Emotional words are used in marketing to connect with consumers on a deeper level by evoking specific emotions or feelings.

Marketers use emotional words to create an emotional response that can drive action or engagement, making their brand more memorable and impactful than a purely logical appeal.

For example, a brand that wants to promote its commitment to customer service might use emotional words like "caring," "attentive," and "responsive" to appeal to consumers who value personalized and attentive customer service.

Using Emotion In Marketing

Emotional words can be used in various marketing channels, such as advertising copy, social media posts, product descriptions, email marketing, and more. When used effectively, emotional words can help create an emotional bond between a brand and its audience, making consumers more likely to choose that brand over others.

It's important to use emotional words thoughtfully and carefully, as they can evoke strong emotions in readers and may have unintended consequences if misused. Additionally, marketers need to be authentic and truthful in using emotional words, as consumers are increasingly wary of brands that engage in emotional manipulation or exaggeration.

Use these powerful words to write compelling content that evokes your intended audience's emotional changes, connections, and responses. These words influence behavior to help convert your prospects into buyers. Here's what's included:

- Encouraging words
- Fear-based words
- Anger-based words
- Safety-based words
- Greed-based words
- Taboo words
- Lust-based words

e.g., Power words in use

Emotional power words are potent tools for tapping into your audience's emotions, connecting them to your message, and driving them to act. Here are a few examples of how emotional power words can be used effectively in marketing:

1. **Ad Copy:** "Unleash your creativity with our groundbreaking design software." Power words: *Unleash, inner, creativity, groundbreaking*
2. **Email Subject Line:** "Unlock exclusive savings on your next dream vacation!" Power words: *Unlock, exclusive, savings, dream*
3. **Blog Post Title:** "10 Proven Strategies to Skyrocket Your Productivity Today" Power words: *Proven, skyrocket, productivity, today*
4. **Social Media Post:** "Transform your workspace with our stunning, eco-friendly office essentials." Power words: *Transform, stunning, eco-friendly, essentials*
5. **Landing Page Headline:** "Discover the Secret to Effortless Weight Loss with Our Revolutionary Program" Power words: *Discover, secret, effortless, revolutionary*
6. **Call-to-Action:** "Join our community of passionate, ambitious entrepreneurs today!" Power words: *Join, community, passionate, ambitious*
7. **Product Description:** "Indulge in our luxurious, handcrafted skincare products for a radiant complexion." Power words: *Indulge, luxurious, handcrafted, radiant*

Remember that using emotional power words effectively means choosing words that resonate with your target audience's desires, fears, or aspirations. By incorporating these words into your marketing, you can evoke strong emotions that help persuade your audience and inspire them to take action.

Real-world pop-culture examples

Here are some real-world examples of emotional power words in marketing from well-known brands and campaigns that have successfully connected with their audiences:

L'Oréal: "Because You're Worth It"
Power words: Worth

This empowering slogan appeals to the audience's desire for self-worth and confidence. L'Oréal's message suggests that using their products is a way to invest in oneself, making it a strong example of emotional marketing.

Dove: "Real Beauty"
Power words: Real, Beauty

Dove's "Real Beauty" campaign promotes self-acceptance and challenging beauty standards. The power words "real" and "beauty" create a sense of authenticity and empowerment, resonating with the audience's desire to embrace their true selves.

McDonald's: "I'm Lovin' It"
Power words: Lovin'

This catchy McDonald's slogan uses the power word "lovin'" to create a positive, emotional association with their brand. It suggests that enjoying McDonald's food is an experience that brings happiness and satisfaction.

These examples demonstrate how emotional power words can effectively create memorable and impactful marketing campaigns that resonate with the target audience.

Encouraging Power Words

- amazing
- perfect
- remarkable
- courageous
- excite
- spectacular
- unbelievable
- grateful
- life-changing
- blissful
- adorable
- magical
- striking
- strong
- powerful
- embolden
- refreshing
- affirming
- awesome
- brilliant
- kudos
- masterful
- breathtaking
- radiant
- fulfilling
- grit
- badass
- phenomenal
- brave
- legendary
- staggering
- fantastic
- delightful
- revitalizing
- stimulating
- reassuring

Encouragement-based power words inspire motivation and confidence in the audience, pushing them to take action and pursue their goals. Words like "believe," "achieve," and "empower."

Fear-Based Power Words

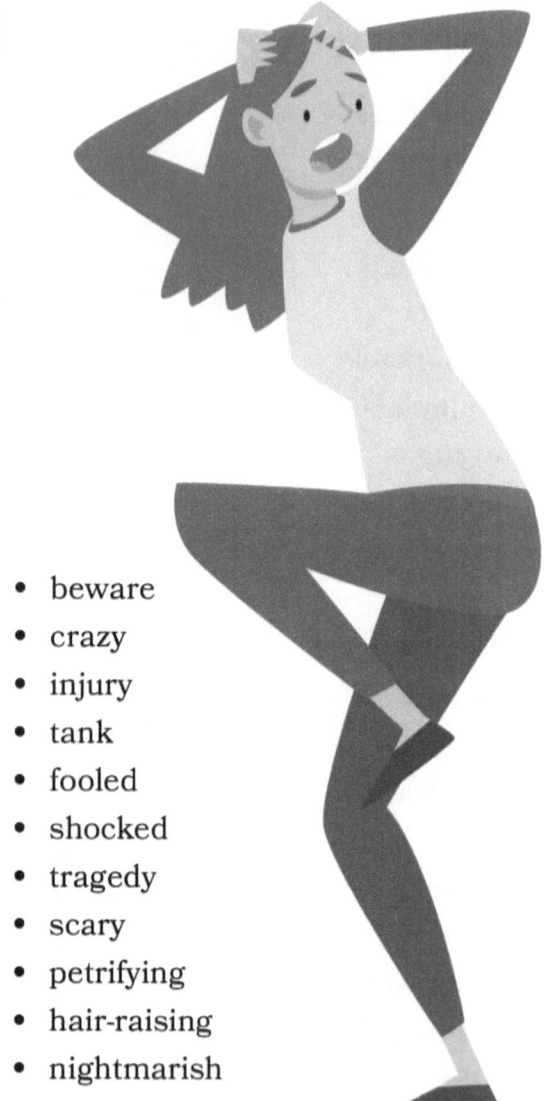

- fail
- mistake
- wreaking havoc
- caution
- teetering
- disastrous
- deadly
- hack
- dangerous
- terror
- hazardous
- panic
- frantic
- victim
- tailspin
- terrifying
- dreadful
- unsettling
- last chance
- doom
- toxic
- agony
- hoax
- worry
- horrific
- beware
- crazy
- injury
- tank
- fooled
- shocked
- tragedy
- scary
- petrifying
- hair-raising
- nightmarish

Fear-based power words tap into the audience's anxieties and insecurities, prompting them to seek solutions that alleviate their concerns. Words like "urgent," "deadline," and "risk."

Anger-Based Power Words

- obnoxious
- cheat
- no good
- foul
- thug
- revolting
- BS
- back-stabbing
- agitating
- slay
- snob
- rude
- slanderous
- spoiled
- rant
- infuriating
- unfair
- exasperating
- phony
- greedy
- rant
- annoying
- weak
- violent
- morally bankrupt
- misleading
- freaking out
- misleading
- full of sh*t
- exploit
- livid
- broke
- sneaky
- maddening
- provoking
- outrageous

Anger-based power words tap into the audience's frustrations and feelings of injustice, prompting them to take action and seek solutions. Words like "unfair," "outrage," and "injustice."

Safety-Based Power Words

- results
- money-back
- tested
- approved
- secure
- reliable
- authority
- world-class
- official
- genuine
- accredited
- well-respected
- endorsed
- studies show
- no strings attached
- stable
- sheltered
- shielded
- track record
- refund
- safe
- certified
- scientifically-proven
- guaranteed
- best-selling
- cancel anytime
- recession-proof
- anonymous
- risk-free
- verifiable
- never fails
- trustworthy
- protected
- defended
- hazard-free

Safety-based power words instill a sense of security and trust, making the audience feel reassured and comfortable with the offered product or service. Words like "guaranteed," "protected," and "certified."

Greed-Based Power Words

- wealth
- peril
- exclusive
- golden
- genius
- booming
- high-paying
- giveaway
- lucky
- effective
- attractive
- hurry
- running out
- running out
- skyrocket
- materialistic
- covetousness
- money
- special
- cheatsheet
- best
- rich
- luxurious
- turbo-charge
- instantly
- never again
- big
- fortune
- six-figure
- upsell
- ahead of the game
- elite
- opportunism
- selfishness

Greed-based power words stimulate the audience's desires for wealth and exclusivity, urging action to seize opportunities. Words like "exclusive," "limited," "bonus," "discount," "profit," "save," and "bargain." These words capitalize on aspirations and the fear of missing out, enticing engagement with your product or service.

Taboo Power Words

- undisclosed
- hilarious
- spoiler
- psycho
- sealed
- top secret
- unheard of
- elusive
- confession
- off the record
- banned
- myth
- hidden
- secret
- insider
- unofficially
- incredible
- unexpected
- insane
- trade secret
- classified
- be the first
- never seen before
- members only
- bizarre
- controversial
- off-limits
- unexplained
- key
- unlock
- behind the scenes
- divisive

Taboo-based power words evoke curiosity and intrigue, touching on controversial or provocative subjects. Words like "forbidden," "confidential," and "insider."

Lust-Based Power Words

- satisfying
- mouthwatering
- enchanting
- passionate
- sensual
- luscious
- compelling
- kinky
- pleasurable
- tantalizing
- hottest
- ecstasy
- longing
- forbidden
- exposed
- risque
- vulgar
- alluring
- orgasmic

- spank
- tease
- naked
- goosebumps
- obsession
- hypnotic
- magnetic
- steamy
- flirt
- wild
- sneak peek

Lust-based power words appeal to the audience's desires and fantasies, creating an allure that drives them to seek out the product or service. Words like "indulge," "temptation," and "irresistible."

Emotions help us connect

This section emphasized the importance of tapping into the emotions of your ideal client to create a deep connection and drive them to take action.

By incorporating "power words" that evoke specific emotions, you can enhance the persuasiveness of your messages and make your content more engaging and memorable.

This chapter provided a starting list of emotional power words, categorized according to the emotions they evoke. These categories included fear, encouragement, safety, taboo, lust, and anger.

Each emotional category uniquely influences the audience's decision-making process, and understanding how to utilize them effectively is vital to crafting compelling marketing messages.

By leveraging the power of these emotion-evoking words, marketers can craft impactful and persuasive messages that resonate with their target audience. Utilizing emotional power words in marketing communication helps create a deeper connection with prospects, compelling them to take action and drive success for your marketing campaigns.

CHAPTER NINE

Get Keyword Smart

In today's competitive landscape, creating captivating content is vital. This chapter covers crafting compelling marketing copy, focusing on strategically using keywords and emotional words in headlines, hashtags, SEO, and SEO-friendly links.

I'll discuss engaging your audience, evoking emotions, and inspiring action through carefully chosen words. Learn to create attention-grabbing headlines that foster emotional connections and keep readers invested.

I'll also explore keywords' crucial role in SEO, ensuring content visibility and driving organic traffic. Optimizing with relevant keywords will improve search engine rankings and establish brand credibility.

Finally, I'll discuss developing persuasive, keyword-rich links that encourage click-throughs and engagement while maintaining a user-friendly experience.

By the chapter's end, you'll have tools and insights to create compelling marketing copy, leveraging keywords and emotional words to enhance your online presence and drive conversions.

Let's dive in and unlock your marketing potential!

Keyword Access

As a content creator, it's crucial to know the words your ideal clients are using when searching online. And thanks to Google and other tools, it's a simpler task than you might imagine!

Google has already gathered all of the data for you. Your job is to collect and use it.

Knowing their search keywords is vital because you want to include these words in your content, hashtags, and social media posts' captions. This allows the algorithms to capture and display your content to the right audience. Or to show up in your ideal client's search results and drive traffic to your content.

Great places to begin your keyword research

- Google Trends
- SEMrush *My personal favorite*
- Ubersuggest

Craft Brilliant Headlines
especially for email subject lines and blog titles

I bet you'd like to do even more to up your social media, email, and blog game. Then listen up! You might already know that subject lines and hooks are critical when engaging your audience. But did you know that there are tools out there that can help you craft hooks and subject lines that resonate with your ideal client?

These tools are tied to data from millions of customer interactions with social media, search engines, emails, and blogs, so you can be confident that you're not shooting in the dark. Gone are the days of running in random directions and hoping to achieve your goals – now, you can use the tools at your disposal to get results.

So you don't have to leave your social media hooks, email subject lines, or blog article titles to chance. With the help of these powerful tools, you can craft subject lines that grab your reader's attention and drive engagement. Give these a try and watch your email and blog performance soar!

Expert tools to help write headlines that sell

- coschedule.com
- optinmonster.com
- subjectline.com
- hubspot.com/blog-topic-generator

Links as blog entry-exit points

Linking to and from your blog posts is crucial in enhancing your website's visibility, credibility, and overall user experience. Inbound links (links from external websites pointing to your content) signal to search engines that your content is valuable and relevant, improving your site's search engine rankings and driving organic traffic. Furthermore, outbound links (links from your content to external websites) provide your readers with additional resources, establishing your blog as a knowledgeable and reliable source of information and building trust with your audience.

Additionally, interlinking (linking to other relevant posts within your blog) helps create a cohesive and easy-to-navigate experience for your readers, encouraging them to explore more of your content and increasing user engagement. This interconnected web of content keeps your audience on your site longer. It helps search engines better understand your website's structure and identify the most critical pages, improving your SEO performance. Ultimately, a well-planned linking strategy enhances the value of your blog, bolsters your online presence, and drives long-term growth for your website.

Examples of places where links matter:

- Keywords should be used within your site to create links to relevant products you want to promote.
- Use keywords when interlinking within your web pages and blog articles to help SEO and direct traffic to your products.
- Include a keyword-rich link that's a call to action (CTA) with *every blog post*. This entices site visitors to opt into your mailing list or buy a relevant product on sale.
- Guest blogging on a partner site showcases your expertise and can deliver keyword-rich links to your site or online store.
- Linking to reputable sites improves SEO and increases brand credibility.

Blog posts & SEO-friendly links

Below, I've provided examples of blog post sentences with SEO-friendly links embedded. In this example, the blog is for a shoe store. In these examples, the SEO-friendly links are embedded using the keywords "**wedges**," "**stilettos**," and "**sneakers**," allowing for better search engine optimization and improved visibility for the shoe store's blog content.

- "Discover the perfect balance of style and comfort with our stunning collection of [wedges](keyword-rich link), featuring a wide variety of colors, materials, and designs to complement any outfit."

- "Step up your fashion game with our elegant and eye-catching [stilettos](keyword-rich link), meticulously crafted to elevate your style and make a bold statement wherever you go."

- "Experience ultimate comfort and unbeatable style with our premium selection of [sneakers](keyword-rich link), perfect for active lifestyles, casual outings, or simply making a fashion statement."

Here's the full blog post as an example:

In the world of footwear, it's essential to have versatile options that cater to your diverse style needs. Whether you're attending a glamorous event, running errands, or exploring the great outdoors, there's a perfect shoe for every occasion. In this blog post, we'll delve into three popular types of footwear – stilettos, sneakers, and wedges – and discuss how each can elevate your style game.

Step up your fashion game with our elegant and eye-catching [stilettos] (*keyword-rich link*), meticulously crafted to elevate your style and make a bold statement wherever you go. These iconic shoes are synonymous with sophistication and femininity, making them the perfect choice for formal events or a night out on the town. Pair them with a little black dress or tailored pants for a chic, polished look that's sure to turn heads.

Experience ultimate comfort and unbeatable style with our premium selection of [sneakers](*keyword-rich link*), perfect for active lifestyles, casual outings, or simply making a fashion statement. Sneakers have evolved from sportswear staples to fashion-forward footwear that combines functionality and style effortlessly. From classic canvas designs to sleek leather options, our sneakers offer diverse styles to suit every taste. Pair them with jeans and a t-shirt for a laid-back weekend look, or dress them up with tailored trousers and a blazer for a trendy, office-appropriate ensemble.

Discover the perfect balance of style and comfort with our stunning collection of [wedges](*keyword-rich link*), featuring various colors, materials, and designs to complement any outfit. Wedges offer the height and elegance of heels without compromising stability and support, making them an excellent choice for daytime and evening wear. Our wedges cater to all fashion preferences, from casual espadrilles to sophisticated suede designs. Pair them with a flowy sundress for a romantic summer look, skinny jeans, and a blouse for a chic, everyday ensemble.

Whether you're a fan of sky-high stilettos, trendy sneakers, or versatile wedges, our shoe store offers a wide selection to suit all your footwear needs. By investing in these three basic styles, you can effortlessly elevate your wardrobe and be prepared for any occasion. So why wait? Explore our diverse range of stilettos, sneakers, and wedges today, and take your style game to new heights.

CHAPTER TEN

Write With Purpose

Hey, it's time to put pen to paper (or fingers to keyboard) and start writing content copy! I know it can be intimidating, but trust me – it doesn't have to be.

This is your chance to speak directly to your perfect customer, connect with them on a deeper level, and address their needs head-on. Remember that ideal client workbook we talked about earlier? Now's the time to put it to use. Think of that one person and speak directly to them.

This is how you establish a connection that resonates.

And don't worry about writing the perfect copy right out of the gate.

Start drafting your ideas and then use the writing tools we discussed earlier to make grammatical and tone edits. Then refine and modify your content until it conveys your intended message and solves the problem you're trying to address for your ideal client.

So don't let the fear of writing hold you back. With a bit of practice and some helpful tips, you'll be crafting killer copy that engages and inspire your audience in no time. So get to it, and happy writing!

Writing Great Copy

Writing is a skill; like any skill, it can be improved with practice. One of the things that have helped me improve my writing skills over the years is using tools like Grammarly. I'll be the first to admit – I have no idea where to put my commas! But with the help of these tools, I've seen a noticeable improvement in the quality of my writing.

So instead of being intimidated by the idea of writing, why not look at it as an opportunity to use these tools and experiences to write excellent copy and improve your skills over time? The more you write, the more comfortable you'll become with the process. And with the help of these tools, you'll be able to craft compelling content that engages and inspires your readers.

So don't let the fear of writing hold you back. Embrace it as an opportunity to learn and grow – and who knows, you might surprise yourself with how much you can achieve.

Great tools to help improve the grammar, SEO, and tone of your writing

- Grammarly
- Hemingway
- Thesaurus.com
- Dictionary.com
- Wordtune
- SEMrush

Once you've made this much progress, all that's needed are tools to keep your writing at a level that showcases your expertise. Here are several grammar and spellcheck tools to help you level up your writing.

- ProWritingAid: a powerful editing tool that can help spot errors, suggest improvements, and enhance your writing.
- WhiteSmoke: a comprehensive grammar, punctuation, and style checker that can help you write better and faster.
- Ginger: an AI-powered grammar and spelling checker that lets you check your writing in real-time.
- AutoCrit: a comprehensive grammar and spelling checker that offers suggestions for improving your writing.
- After The Deadline: an AI-powered writing assistant and grammar checker to help you clean up your writing.
- LanguageTool: a free, open-source grammar and spelling checker that can be used for both English and non-English language documents.
- PaperRater: an online grammar and spelling checker that can help you identify potential errors in your writing.
- Scribens: an AI-powered grammar and spelling checker that can help you improve your writing style.
- Reverso: a free online grammar and spelling checker that can help you quickly and accurately identify potential errors in your writing.

Using AI As A Content Source

Do you know what's super exciting? The way AI is transforming marketing content creation! Imagine advanced algorithms whipping up high-quality content quickly, freeing you up to tackle those big-picture marketing plans. Plus, AI can help craft personalized and targeted content, which means your audience is more likely to engage with what you're putting out there. It's like having a secret weapon in your marketing arsenal!

But let's be honest – AI isn't without its challenges. For one, there's the risk that content might lose that human touch and empathy we all crave. AI can sometimes struggle with understanding those emotional nuances and cultural sensitivities, which might lead to content that doesn't quite hit the mark or even offends your audience. And we can't forget the danger of relying too much on AI, which could stifle our creative juices.

So, how can we make the most of AI in marketing content creation? It's about striking that perfect balance between human creativity and machine efficiency. Use AI to handle those repetitive tasks, but stay involved in the brainstorming and editing processes to keep your brand's voice and values on point. By blending the power of AI with your emotional intelligence and creativity, you'll unlock the true potential of AI-driven marketing content, and that's when the magic happens!

Examples of AI Tools For Content Creation

- OpenAI's GPT-3: OpenAI's GPT-3 is a state-of-the-art language model that can generate human-like text based on a given prompt. It can help create blog posts, social media captions, email copy, and more while maintaining context and coherence.

- Articoolo: An AI-powered content generation tool that can create unique, SEO-optimized articles on various topics. It helps generate blog posts, website content, and marketing materials with minimal effort.

- Copy.ai: An AI content generator designed specifically for marketing purposes. It can help you create persuasive copy, product descriptions, ad headlines, social media content, and more by leveraging the power of AI.

- Kuki Chatbot (*formerly Mitsuku*): A conversational AI chatbot that can assist in creating interactive content for your website, social media, or messaging apps. It enables personalized communication with your audience, leading to better engagement and improved customer experience.

- Phrasee: An AI-driven marketing language generation platform specializing in creating email subject lines and social media ad copy. It helps marketers optimize their content for higher open rates, click-through rates, and conversions.

These are just a few examples of AI tools that can help with marketing content creation. As AI technology advances, the potential applications for content generation will expand, offering more sophisticated and efficient solutions for marketers.

This is the format of a good ChatGPT prompt

- Topic: Benefits of Meditation
- Type of Content: Blog Post
- Target Audience: Young adults interested in mental health and wellness

- Goal of Content: To educate and persuade the target audience on the benefits of meditation for mental health and wellness and encourage them to try it.

Key Points to Include:

- Explanation of what meditation is and how it works
- Scientific evidence supporting the benefits of meditation for mental health and wellness
- Personal anecdotes or testimonials from individuals who have experienced the benefits of meditation
- Practical tips for incorporating meditation into daily life
- Common misconceptions about meditation and why they are not accurate

- Desired Tone: Approachable, informative, and inspiring
- Length: 800-1000 words

Keywords: meditation, mental health, wellness, mindfulness, relaxation, stress reduction, self-care

Additional Notes: Please include at least one relevant image and use subheadings to break up the content for easy reading.

This is the ChatGPT output from that prompt

TITLE: Discovering the Benefits of Meditation: A Guide for Young Adults

SUBHEADINGS:
- What is Meditation, and How Does it Work?
- Scientific Evidence Supporting the Benefits of Meditation
- Personal Testimonials: How Meditation Can Improve Mental Health and Wellness

- Making Meditation Part of Your Daily Routine: Practical Tips
- Debunking Common Misconceptions About Meditation
- Additional Resources for Meditation Practice

IMAGE: A photo of a young adult meditating in a peaceful setting, such as a beach or a park.

BLOG POST: Do you ever feel overwhelmed by daily life? Are you looking for a way to improve your mental health and wellness? Meditation may be just what you need. This ancient practice has been proven to offer many benefits for the mind, body, and soul. In this guide, we will explore the benefits of meditation for young adults interested in mental health and wellness.

What is Meditation, and How Does it Work?

Meditation is the practice of training the mind to achieve a state of calm and relaxation. It involves focusing on the present moment, typically using a specific technique, such as deep breathing, visualization, or mantra repetition. Practicing meditation regularly allows individuals to control their thoughts and emotions, reduce stress and anxiety, and improve overall well-being.

Scientific Evidence Supporting the Benefits of Meditation

Numerous studies have shown that meditation can significantly benefit mental health and wellness. Research has found that meditation can reduce symptoms of anxiety and depression, improve attention and concentration, increase feelings of happiness and well-being, lower blood pressure, and reduce the risk of heart disease.

Personal Testimonials: How Meditation Can Improve Mental Health and Wellness

Many individuals have experienced the benefits of meditation firsthand. For example, Sarah, a 25-year-old marketing manager, started practicing meditation last year and found that it helped her manage her anxiety and stress. "I used to feel like my mind was always racing, but now I feel more in control," she says. "Meditation has become an essential part of my daily routine."

Making Meditation Part of Your Daily Routine: Practical Tips

If you're interested in incorporating meditation into your daily routine, here are some practical tips to get started:

- Find a quiet space: Choose a quiet, comfortable space to focus without distractions.
- Use guided meditations: Use guided meditations to help you stay focused and learn different techniques.
- Be consistent: Make meditation a daily habit to experience the full benefits.

Debunking Common Misconceptions About Meditation

Despite its growing popularity, there are still some common misconceptions about meditation. For example, some believe meditation is only for spiritual or religious people. However, meditation is a secular practice that anyone can benefit from, regardless of their beliefs or background.

Meditation is a powerful tool that can improve mental health, reduce stress, and promote well-being. By incorporating meditation into your daily routine, you can experience the benefits firsthand. So take a deep breath, find a quiet space, and meditate today!

CHAPTER ELEVEN

Autopilot & Efficiency

Let's explore how automation transforms the marketing landscape and uncover new opportunities for businesses to streamline their processes and maximize efficiency.

As a business owner, embracing automation can unlock countless benefits, such as reducing manual workload, increasing accuracy, and improving the overall effectiveness of your marketing efforts.

From email marketing and social media management to lead nurturing and customer relationship management, I'll delve into various categories of automation tools designed to revolutionize your marketing strategies.

So, buckle up and get ready to discover how marketing automation can give your business a competitive edge and free up valuable time for you to focus on what truly matters – growing your business and delighting your customers!

Why Marketing Automation

Email marketing automation tools enable businesses to streamline their email campaigns, making it easier to nurture leads, retain customers, and promote products or services. These tools allow you to create personalized, targeted emails triggered by specific actions or events, such as a new subscriber, a purchase, or a customer's birthday. By automating your email marketing, you can ensure consistent communication with your audience, improve open and click-through rates, and ultimately drive higher conversions.

Managing multiple social media platforms can be time-consuming for business owners. Social media management automation tools help you schedule posts, track engagement, and monitor your brand's online presence more efficiently. These tools allow you to maintain a consistent posting schedule, promptly respond to comments and messages, and analyze your social media performance, resulting in stronger relationships with your audience and increased brand awareness.

Lead nurturing automation tools guide prospects through the sales funnel, turning them from casual visitors into loyal customers. These tools allow you to segment your audience based on their behavior and preferences, enabling you to create highly-targeted marketing campaigns that resonate with each individual. Automating your lead nurturing process can build trust and credibility with your audience, ultimately increasing conversion rates and customer lifetime value.

CRM automation streamlines your interactions with customers and prospects, ensuring a seamless and personalized experience. Tools like Salesforce, Zoho CRM, and Microsoft Dynamics 365 enable you to automate data entry, contact management, and deal-tracking tasks. By centralizing customer information and automating communications, you can better understand your audience, enhance customer satisfaction, and drive sales.

Creating, distributing, and analyzing content is vital to any marketing strategy. Content marketing automation tools like CoSchedule, ClearVoice, and Contently help you plan, produce, and distribute content more efficiently. Automate content ideation, editorial calendar management, and social sharing tasks to ensure a consistent and targeted content strategy that drives engagement and conversions.

Accurate and timely data analysis is essential for making informed marketing decisions. Analytics and reporting automation tools like Google Analytics, Adobe Analytics, and Databox help you collect, visualize, and interpret data from various marketing channels. Automating your analytics and reporting process ensures you receive actionable insights, allowing you to optimize your marketing efforts and make data-driven decisions for your business's growth.

Automation & Scheduling Tools

Below are several reputable **content creation, automation, and scheduling tools**. Most have trial versions. I've bolded the ones I recommend, but choose the ones that feel most intuitive to you.

Email Marketing

- mailchimp.com
- **ChatGPT**
- constantcontact.com
- **hubspot.com/products/marketing/email**
- campaignmonitor.com
- drip.com
- aweber.com

Social Media

- feedly.com
- **canva.com**
- **trends.google.com**
- **neilpatel.com/ubersuggest**
- **hootsuite.com**
- **later.com**
- socedo.com
- sproutsocial.com
- animoto.com
- meetedgar
- sendible

Forms and Surveys

- **typeform.com**
- gravityforms.com
- paperforms.co
- wufoo.com
- **surveymonkey.com**

Customer Relationship Management

- drip.com
- **hubspot.com**
- monday.com
- **zapier.com**
- keap.com
- zoho

Time Management

- todoist.com
- focuskeeper
- toggl
- **onenote**
- slack
- **google drive**
- evernote
- **stayfocusd**

Graphics and Colors

- **coolors.co**
- **canva.com**
- picmonkey.com
- colorhunt.io
- unspalsh.com
- **stock.adobe.com**
- **istockphoto.com**

Copywriting and SEO

- **grammarly.com**
- hemmingwayapp.com
- **ChatGPT**
- **subjectline.com**
- buzzsumo.com
- **yoast.com** (*WordPress sites*)
- answerthepublic.com
- emailsubjectlinegrader.com
- spamcheck.postmarkapp.com
- **coshedule.com/headline-analyzer**

APPENDIX
ROADMAP AND BEST PRACTICES

Your 11-Step Roadmap

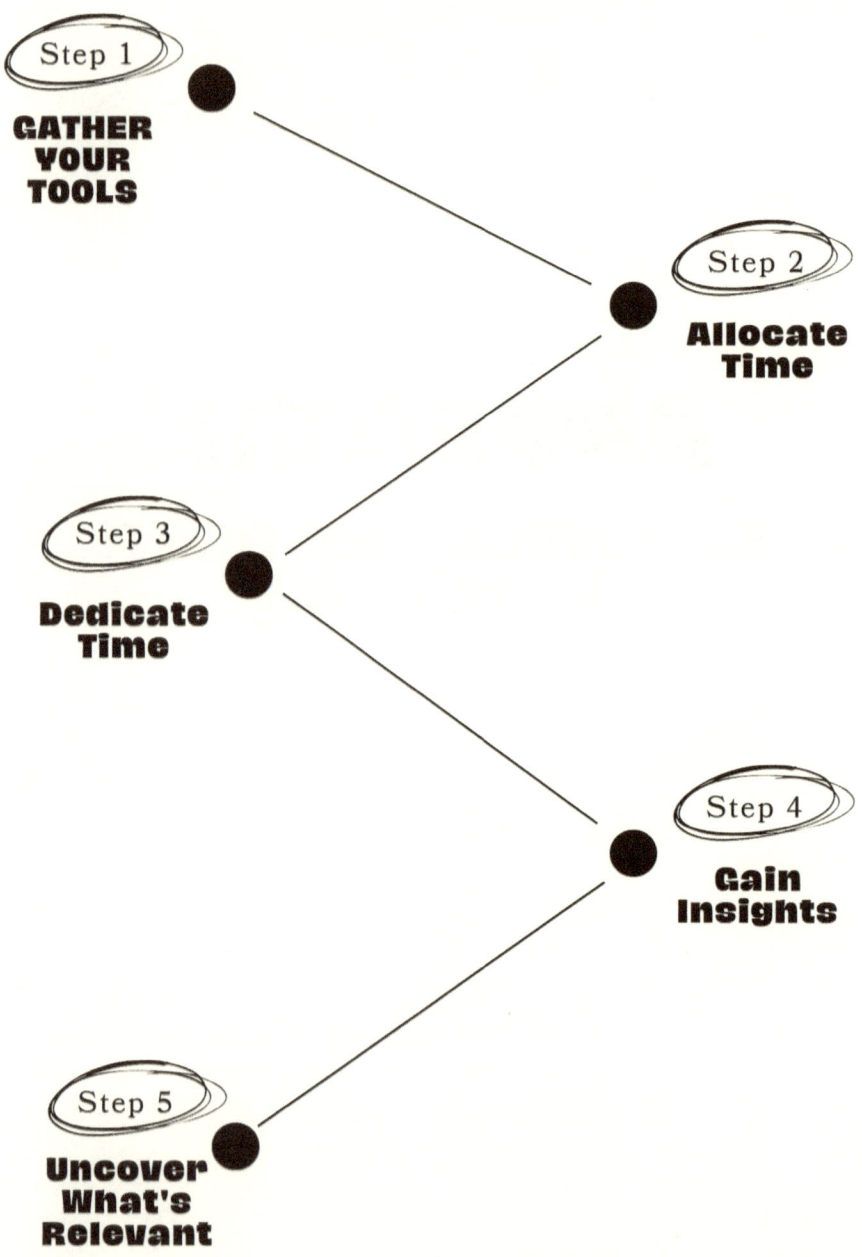

- **Step 1** — GATHER YOUR TOOLS
- **Step 2** — Allocate Time
- **Step 3** — Dedicate Time
- **Step 4** — Gain Insights
- **Step 5** — Uncover What's Relevant

USE YOUR ROADMAP | 81

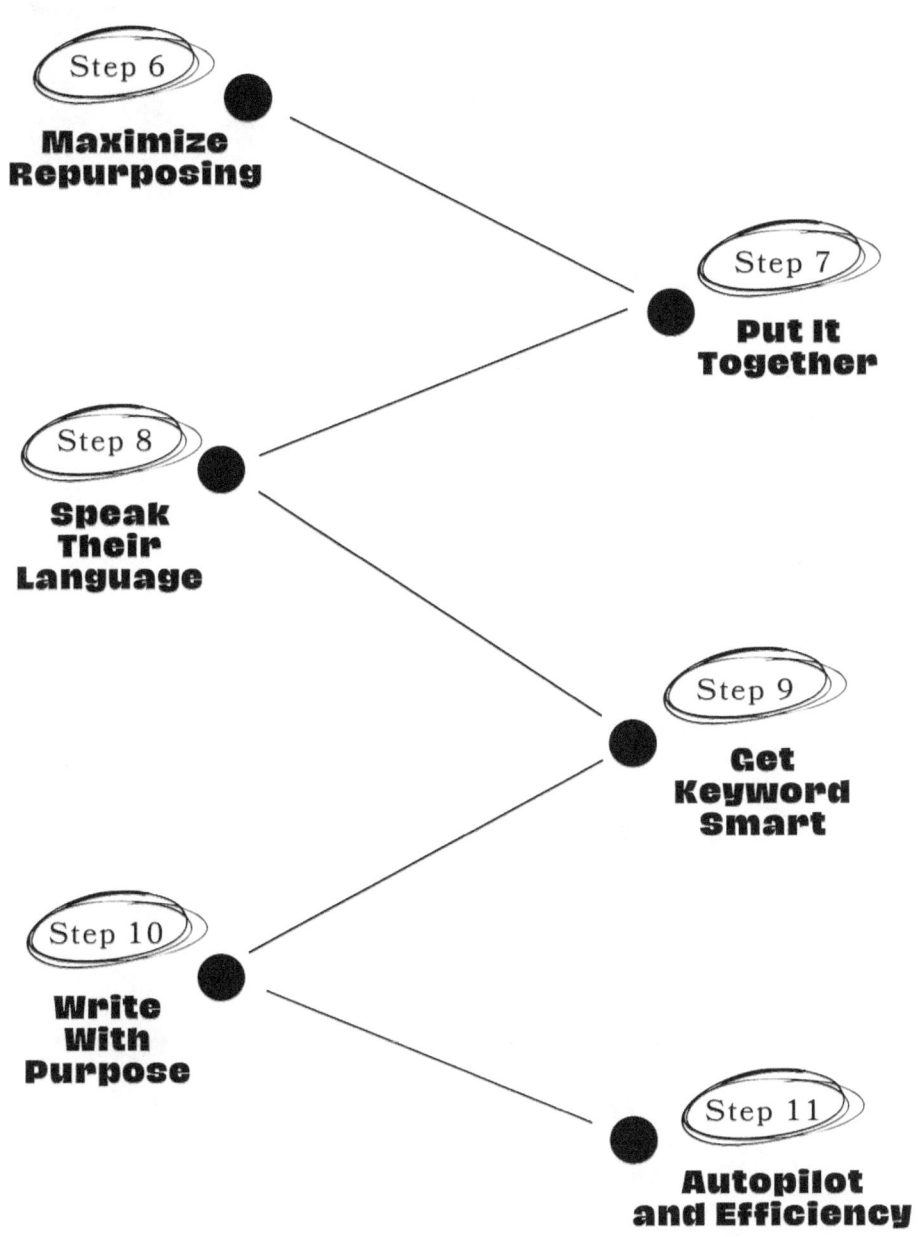

Best Practices

Email Marketing: "*Forty-seven percent of email recipients open an email based on the subject line.*" — Zippia.com

- Keep email subject lines at 30 to 50 characters.
- Personalize the subject lines and email messages.
- Make your emails intriguing to your ideal prospects by using "power words" or asking questions.
- Don't guess what to write. Instead, choose topics based on your research findings and what you know about your ideal prospects.

Blog Posts: "*Seventy-one percent of bloggers say SEO is the most important traffic source.*" — Orbitmedia.com

- Write how-tos... that your ideal prospects find relevant
- Write relevant product reviews that benefit your ideal prospects
- Intrigue your ideal prospects by using power words or questions in your titles
- Get SEO- friendly by including researched keywords your ideal prospects use.

Website: "*Seventy-one percent of businesses now have a website in 2023. This is an increase from previous years.*" — TopDesignFirms

- Make sure it's mobile-friendly and easy to navigate from the perspective of your ideal prospect.
- Update content regularly.
- Include a call-to-actions on every page.

Social Media: "*The number of social media users globally grew from 4.2 billion in January 2021 to 4.62 billion in January 2022 — a 10.1% growth year-over-year.*" — Smartinsights.com

- Show up regularly and be consistent.
- Have a full bio showing visitors you are an authentic business.
- Be easily spotted among the noise by being consistent with your brand look and tone.
- Don't guess what to post. Instead, choose topics based on your research findings and what you know about your ideal prospects.

Congratulations!

Congratulations on finishing Create Killer Content! By reading this book, you've taken a significant step towards improving your marketing efforts and growing your business.

But don't let your efforts end here. It's now time to take action by using the knowledge you've gained to create a plan of action for your business. Put in the effort and time needed to research your ideal client, create compelling content, and distribute it strategically.

Remember, creating compelling content that resonates with your ideal client takes time and effort, but the payoff is worth it. By consistently delivering valuable content that speaks to the needs and interests of your ideal client, you'll build trust, establish your brand as an authority and ultimately, grow your business.

So, take a deep breath, get ready to roll up your sleeves, and put what you've learned into action. I believe in the possibilities that exist for you, and I'm excited to see your business flourish with the power of strategic content marketing.

**Ready to take charge
of your marketing?**
Learn more at
www.marciahylton.com

www.ingramcontent.com/pod-product-compliance
Lightning Source LLC
Chambersburg PA
CBHW020448220526
45464CB00002B/906